FEMINIST RYAN GOSLING

As Imagined

Feminist Theory ^
from Your Favorite Sensitive
Movie Dude

Danielle Henderson

RUNNING PRESS
PHILADELPHIA · LONDON

Disclaimer

This book is a work of humor. It was not authorized, prepared, approved, licensed, or endorsed by Ryan Gosling, or anyone on his behalf, nor does it reflect his actual views—as far as we know.

Books published by Running Press are available at special discounts for bulk purchases in the United States by corporations, institutions, and other organizations. For more information, please contact the Special Markets Department at the Perseus Books Group, 2300 Chestnut Street, Suite 200, Philadelphia, PA 19103, or call (800) 810-4145, ext. 5000, or e-mail special.markets@perseusbooks.com.

ISBN 978-0-7624-4736-7
Library of Congress Control Number: 2012931370

E-book ISBN 978-0-7624-4751-0

9   8   7   6   5
Digit on the right indicates the number of this printing

Cover and interior design by Jason Kayser
Edited by Jordana Tusman
Typography: Minion

Running Press Book Publishers
2300 Chestnut Street
Philadelphia, PA 19103-4371

Visit us on the web!
www.runningpress.com
www.feministryangosling.tumblr.com

Dedication

For my grandma, Carole, who taught
me how to throw a punch.

Introduction

When I started the Feminist Ryan Gosling blog, I was a newly minted, academically frustrated graduate student looking for an outlet. Now, nearly a year later, I am an academically frustrated graduate student who *started giving herself additional homework* in the form of writing this book.

Theory gets dense and boring very quickly. My friends and I were learning up to ten new theorists a week, and keeping track of them was starting to wear us out—not in the typical, lazy college student we-don't-want-to-work-this-hard sort of way, but in the overworked, underprepared holy-shit-is-the-human-brain-supposed-to-function-like-this sort of way. I needed a break.

My husband and I went to see *Drive*. Since I hadn't engaged with the outside world in months, I didn't know what the movie was about, but I knew it wasn't about Michel Foucault, and that was good enough for me.

For the next few days, I had Ryan Gosling on the brain as I slogged through Steinem, Lacan, and Kahlo. I had revenge fantasies in the style of the film where I quivered above my textbooks with a hammer and nail. Remembering a meme I had seen a few months prior, I found a few photos of Ryan Gosling's face, splashed them with thoughts based on my actual homework, and posted them on a blog in an effort to cheer up my friends. Just a little something to help us study.

I greatly underestimated the power of Ryan Gosling's face.

The blog that was originally intended for five people started appearing on news sources overnight. People were following, commenting, and reposting the pictures on their Facebook walls by the thousands. It was deeply weird, but also a little exciting. *People were interested in feminist theory.*

Normally when I tell people I'm a gender studies major, they look at me like I'm studying Sanskrit or Latin. But now, NOW I had something to show my family, to possibly convince them that one day I would be employable. *Look! People still like feminism!* Or maybe they just really like Ryan Gosling's face. *But they're getting that face with a dose of feminism! Like it or not.*

There's no way to tell if Ryan Gosling is actually a feminist; feminism is serious business, and something you have to come to on your own terms. He hasn't actually said anything in this book. But he is charming, talented, and intelligent; he has said some things in the media that can be construed as feminist. He loves his mom and takes ballet. He has nice things to say about the women he dates. It's not too far-fetched, right?

The response to the website has been overwhelmingly positive, and one of the coolest parts is getting e-mail from people who are new to feminism or feminist theory asking, "Who are you talking about?" I don't expect that you'll know every name mentioned in this book—I certainly didn't know a lot of them last year. But I'm a teacher by trade, and I do hope your curiosity incites you to ~~pick up an encyclopedia~~ Google them to find out.

This is a book about feminist theory, sure. But for every mention of Foucault and Friedan, there's an Amy Poehler or Margaret Cho. Theory starts to make sense when you find a way to make it jive with your own life. The "hey girl" is pejorative on purpose and is part of the original meme. I thought the juxtaposition was pretty hilarious when coupled with a block of dense feminist text. I'm not making fun *of* feminism; I'm having fun *with* feminism.

I hope you enjoy the book and are able to do the same.

Hey girl.

The post-feminist fetishization of motherhood is deeply rooted in classism, but I still think we'd make cute babies.

Hey girl.

We don't need arbitrary beauty archetypes steeped in historically biased ideologies pumped out to us by mediocre forms of media to define our sexiness.

Hey girl.

Julia Kristeva
talks about
love being
the modern
obscenity
like she was
spying on us
last night.

Hey girl.
We can't smash
the patriarchy without
the right tools.

Hey girl.

This pick-up game is okay, but I wish we were courtside watching Lisa Leslie take it to the rim instead.

Hey girl.

All I want for my birthday is a subscription to *Ms. Magazine*.

Hey girl.

You've torn
down the
yellow wallpaper
of my soul.

Hey girl.

Yeah, but when he said, "Breastfeeding in public is offensive," was the crew from *Punk'd* standing behind him?

Hey girl.

Start a revolution—stop hating your body.

Hey girl.

Derrida thinks language
is fluid enough to
break the gender divide,
but I can't imagine a
world where we could
get even closer.

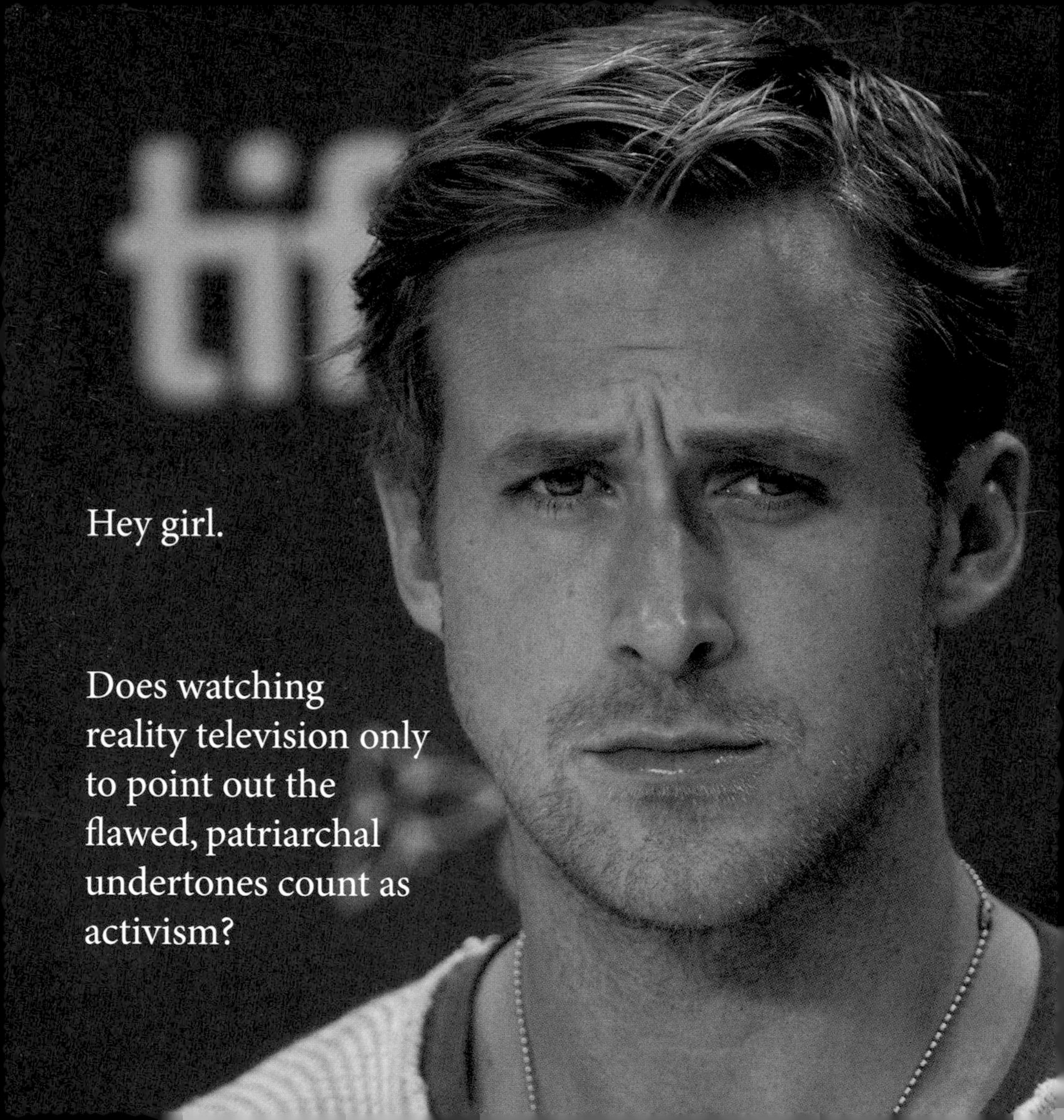
Hey girl.
Does watching reality television only to point out the flawed, patriarchal undertones count as activism?

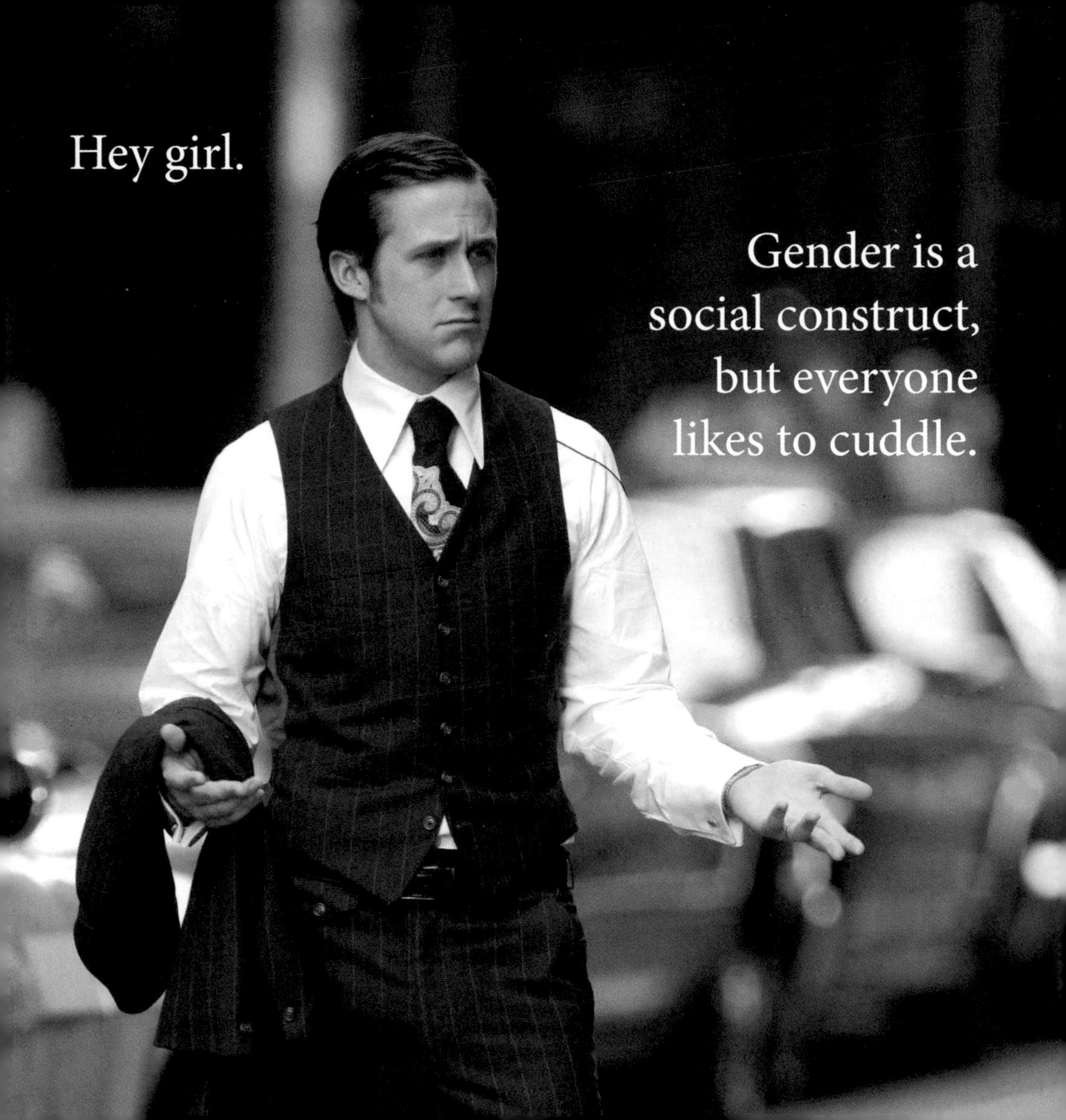
Hey girl.
Gender is a social construct, but everyone likes to cuddle.

Hey girl.

How many consecutive episodes of *Xena* are too many?

Hey girl.

I agree with
Chandra Mohanty
that Western feminism
has a problem with
referring to women as
"third world," since
all women are
No. 1 in my heart.

Hey girl.

I mean ...
WOMAN.

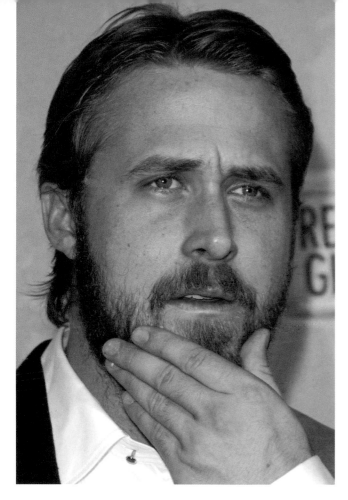

Hey girl.

Is there a merit badge for transcending normative cultural beliefs about femininity?

Hey girl.

At least 90 percent of the pieces in this exhibit could use the Guerilla Girls treatment.

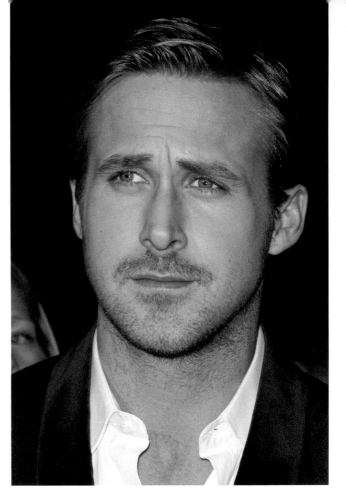

Hey girl.

I believe Foucault's
theory of marriage is a
governmentally developed
tool that interferes
with the appropriation
of land rights and normalizes
heterosexuality, but I
still want to spend the rest
of my life with you.

Hey girl.

I hope this is over soon—there's a box of brownies and a Margaret Cho DVD at home with my name all over them.

Hey girl.

Just daydreaming about what a kick-ass, crime-fighting duo Emma Goldman and I would make.

Hey girl.

Hollywood may struggle with developing content that advocates feminism or promotes stories with strong female leads, but at least Joss Whedon is on our side.

Hey girl.

We can be supportive of gender variance even while we get our bounce on.

Hey girl.

Mr. Rochester might be a misunderstood character, but it's still messed up that he would keep any woman locked in an attic.

Hey girl.

It's been a tough week; do you want to just stay in tonight, rub bellies, and talk about Derrida's politics of sexual difference?

Hey girl.

In the words of
Dean Spade, "Dress to
kill, fight to win."

Hey girl.

Despite what
TV commercials
show you, I
totally know
how to wash dishes,
do my laundry,
and cook.

Hey girl.

I don't disagree with Brah's assessment of transnational migration altering the power structure and changing the political economy of women by creating new diasporas expressed as concepts, discourses, and experiences— I just want you to move in so we can spend more time together.

Hey girl.

Listening
to Julia Serano
talk about trans
feminism makes
me positively
giddy.

Hey girl.

My eyes are up here.

Hey girl.

Since you make $0.77 for every dollar I earn, I'm happy to pay for the movie tickets tonight.

Hey girl.

Women make
up 51 percent of
the U.S. population
and only 17 percent
of the government,
but you're the
commander in chief
of my heart.

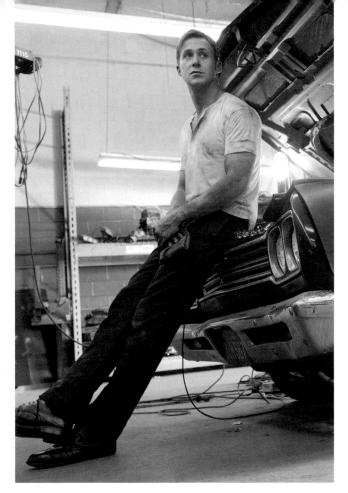

Hey girl.

We could keep talking about post-structuralists and their engagement with narrative, but I thought it would be fun to go home, get in bed, and watch some *Buffy*.

Hey girl.

Bella Abzug had a hat for every occasion, but do you think I can do the look justice?

Hey girl.

Sharpen your pencil—I just got the go-ahead to teach only the works of Octavia Butler from now until I retire.

Hey girl.

Anne Fausto-Sterling
has a theory that
five categorical sexes
would help break
constrictive gender
norms, but the only sex
I need is yours.

Hey girl.

Betty Friedan called it "the problem with no name," but I call it the patriarchy.

Hey girl.

Nolite te bastardes carborundorum.

Hey girl.

I just think
Spinderella is
underrated
as an innovator
and stylistic
collaborator.

Hey girl.

Your research project should TOTALLY be a qualitative analysis of feminist representations on TV comparing Tami Taylor's religiously influenced south to Loreleigh Gilmore's financially structured north!

Hey girl.

Since you have the dual burden of working both in and outside of the home and the social stigma attached to choosing both or either, why don't you let me make dinner tonight?

Hey girl.

I support your right to choose what happens to your body without government intervention.

Hey girl.

Keep your laws
off my body, but keep
your hands on it.

Hey girl.

I think educational reform should begin and end with Queen Latifah's "U.N.I.T.Y." blasting over the loudspeaker at the start and close of every school day.

Hey girl.

We don't call our sisters *bitches*.

Hey girl.

You look like
such a badass
when you step up
to the mic.

Hey girl.

Being a guest on *The Rachel Maddow Show* might be a pipe dream, but it's my happy place.

Hey girl.

The ultimate adventure movie would have been a documentary of Florynce Kennedy and Gloria Steinem hitting the lecture circuit.

Hey girl.

My only plans this weekend involve hanging out with my dog, shooting some hoops, and trying to directly combat the devaluation of young women by watching a few episodes of *Smart Girls at the Party*.

Hey girl.

But maybe Hermione, with her pro-feminist stance and emerging activism, was *really* the hero of the story?

Hey girl.

If they're looking for a way to successfully implement employer-provided childcare, why can't they just watch *9 to 5* again?

Hey girl.

The cultural impetus to make women feel ashamed of taking pleasure in sex is rooted in a power differential that gives preference to male satisfaction— but I'm not that insecure.

Hey girl.

Wouldn't it be awesome if Felicia Day were part of our D&D campaign?

Hey girl.

Just getting my gear ready to teach at Girls Rock Camp this summer.

Hey girl.

I guess Wangari Mathaai received a Nobel Peace Prize because they haven't yet created one for international human rights environmental feminist trailblazing yet.

Hey girl.

Susan B. Anthony had a good run, so maybe it's time to put America Ferrara on the dollar coin.

Hey girl.

I try to use my
male privilege
for good,
but it still sucks
that I have so
much of it.

Hey girl.

We'd be more successful at reclaiming public space for women if we were willing to address the patriarchal fixtures that made it unsafe in the first place.

Hey girl.

Wait—so, Frieda Kahlo was an important figure in Chicana feminism whose legacy incites women to share their personal narrative through expressive artistic endeavors AND she had a pet monkey?

Hey girl.

You built a room of
your own and a room
in my heart.

Hey girl.

I'm pretty psyched for the chance to make a movie that passes the Bechdel Test.

Hey girl.

I am staying.
On this bench.
Until Le Tigre.
Makes another
album.

Hey girl.

I'm just a little sad that I never got to be a guest on *Oprah*.

Hey girl.

Just listening to you talk about Patricia Hill Collins' matrix of domination as an ideological tool that reveals the hegemonic social structure makes me thank my lucky stars for you.

Hey girl.

I know that Luce Irigaray is deeply into some Jacques Lacan–type stuff with regards to a critique of the masculine subject, but I thought she'd go out with me anyway.

Hey girl.

Let's start
our own sexual
revolution.

Hey girl.

The Equal Rights Amendment hasn't been adopted, but thousands of people are taking to the streets for a *FOOTBALL* victory?

71

Hey girl.

Be cool—
I think that's
Carrie Brownstein.

Hey girl.

No, actually, I *do not* understand why there hasn't been a statue created in Amy Poehler's honor.

Hey girl.

I'm working
on a plan
to stretch
International
Women's Day
into an entire
year.

Hey girl.

Anyone questioning the power of the female voice clearly hasn't heard you give a presentation to the budget committee.

Hey girl.

Does compulsory heterosexuality require that I be *more* or *less* like Prince?

Hey girl.

When Foucault
asks whether
or not we
need a theory
of power, he's
clearly never met
YOUR badass.

Hey girl.

Oh my god,
Pam Grier is here!

Hey girl.

It's probably not what Gloria Steinem had in mind, but let's count our refusal to define this relationship by traditional standards as an everyday rebellion.

Hey girl.

I know that Elizabeth Grosz thinks the body is a surface upon which law, morality, and values are inscribed, but my body is really into hanging out with yours as much as possible.

Hey girl.

I think
I'm more of
a Khadijah
to your
Maxine.

Hey girl.

Let's get out of here. He's doing that annoying thing again where he suggests that all women are obsessed with shoes and diamonds.

Hey girl.

Jabba's imprisonment of Leia was *totally* a metaphor for patriarchal fear of politically effective female military leaders!

Hey girl.

If one more person tries to convince me that government has any business dictating reproductive options for women, I will drive this car into a wall.

Hey girl.

If Anna Julia Cooper could transcend slave-born boundaries, rewrite school books to remove racist text, earn a Ph.D. from the Sorbonne, and live to be over one hundred years old, I'm pretty sure I can make it through this dissertation committee meeting unscathed.

Hey girl.

Anyone who undervalues women in sciences has never seen you sterilize with an autoclave.

Hey girl.

Let's take back
the night.

Hey girl.

Women's rights ARE
civil rights.

Hey girl.

Perhaps Aretha Franklin's "Respect" wouldn't be such a mainstay if more people had figured out how to be more inclusive of women's rights in the four decades since the song was released.

Hey girl.

I was going to go to the gym, but we've still got some *Gilmore Girls* episodes on the DVR.

Hey girl.

The patriarchal establishment may fail to give a voice to women's issues, but I could spend hours talking with you.

Hey girl.

I finally got a copy of
Out of the Vinyl Deeps so
I can talk about Ellen
Willis' ability to infuse
pop culture with political
critiques through a feminist
lens with you.

Hey girl.

Say what you will about *Sex and the City*, but I maintain that *Golden Girls* was the most feminist show ever featured on television.

Hey girl.

A woman's role as caregiver is not biologically determined.

Hey girl.

Listening to you talk about the evolution of government-sanctioned sexism is my kind of consciousness-raising.

Hey girl.

I still can't believe
Artemesia Genteleschi's
paintings just *hang*
in museums like we're
worthy of seeing
them.

Hey girl.

Wittig's definition of phallogocentric culture may be key to redefining feminism, but do you think she would've liked my movies?

Hey girl.

I know how Barbara Smith feels about feminism and the need for autonomy, but does that mean we can't go to karaoke together?

Hey girl.

I literally have no idea how to react to someone who hasn't read Judy Blume's *Forever*.

Hey girl.

Audre Lorde says
we can't use the
master's tools
to dismantle the
master's house, but
I say we blast some
Black Sabbath
and find out.

Hey girl.

I believe in health at any size—all bodies are good bodies.

Hey girl.

Oh, when you said we were going to a dinner party, I thought you meant the one by Judy Chicago at the Brooklyn Museum.

Hey girl.

I can't have a realistic conversation about the representation of women in comics with someone who hasn't even read the Maggie and Hopey stories in *Love and Rockets*.

Hey girl.

I know you're worried since Germaine Greer argues that the suburban nuclear family contributes to women being detached from their sexuality, but we're still in the city limits if we just move across town.

Hey girl.

I'm presenting a paper on the impact of revolutionary Latina experiences on second wave feminism using dialectical methodology to discuss Cherríe Moraga's autobiographical prose—but is this really the right suit for it?

Hey girl.

I *totally*
just tripped
in front
of Kathleen
Hanna!

Hey girl.

It's hard for me
to reify de Beauvoire's
theory of lost
female genius when
I'm around you.

Hey girl.

Of course I'm voting today—
Lucy Burns didn't picket
the White House
for nothing.

Hey girl.

I was blasting a recording of someone reading the Combahee River Collective Statement on the way over to get pumped up for this rally.

Hey girl.

I do not think the historical legacy of women should be based on their work inside the home, but I'm also sort of in love with those brownies you just whipped up.

Hey Girl.

The hegemonic relationship we have with the prison industrial complex cannot hold if we plan to develop as a nation, but I'll always hold you.

Hey girl.

Riots,
not diets.

Hey girl.

I know how Judith Butler feels about subverting the dominant paradigm and rejecting the naturalization of heteronormativity, but I got you this flower.

Hey girl.

I need to get home to see if Kate Beaton has posted a new comic.

Hey girl.

Let's do some rhetorical analysis of your bedroom.

SENIOR CITIZENS AND
HALF FARE CARD
HOLDERS **MUST** PRESENT VALID
D. CARD FOR **EACH** BOARDING
THANK YOU

Hey girl.

I got you a subscription to *Bitch*
magazine in lieu of a traditional magazine
that presents a one-dimensional view of
beauty, sexuality, and culture.

Hey girl.

We're just trying to figure out if Gloria Anzaldúa's *Borderlands* is theoretically foundational to all discussions of intersectionality, or just those dealing with women of color.

Hey girl.

Hillary Clinton might have
spent the past thirty years being
a leading figure in advocacy
for women and children, but
with intelligence like that,
she's also my No. 1 choice for
right-hand lady in the event of
a zombie attack.

Hey girl.

My perfect Saturday is a hot cup of tea at sunrise, a trip to the farmer's market, and curling up on the couch with you to figure out bell hooks' theory that feminism is a struggle to eradicate the ideology of domination that permeates Western culture.

Hey girl.

If feminist backlash would have people believe that we've done all we can for women's rights, how do you explain Michelle Bachmann?

Hey girl.

I mean *grrl*.

Hey girl.

When people complain
about the dearth of
young women making
waves in the feminist
movement, I just
shout "Tavi Gevinson"
and PEACE OUT
of there.

Hey girl.

This gig is okay, but Gerda Lerner pretty much had my dream job.

Hey girl.

This is what
a feminist looks like.

Photo Credits

Acknowledgments

BIG thanks to: Jordana Tusman, Jason Kayser, Bill Jones, Chris Navratil, Sue Oyama, and everyone at Running Press and Perseus Books Group for your time and support. Grrl Gang Midwest: Elena Lavarreda, Anne Peters, Kelly Fox, Julia Gutierrez, and Mary Durden for ladies' lunches, drinks at Coopers, and revealing the secret relationship between Lacan and Tupac. Grrl Gang East Coast: Alexis Gorton for your science advice, crocheted uteri, and every moment of your friendship for the past two decades. Nelli Ruotsalainen, Melanie Carrazzo, and Anna Vaccaro for holding down the feminist fort in Finland, Boston, and Rhode Island. Sandra Pieloch, Kurt Schlachter, Sarah and Nick Hughes for early e-mails, late phone calls, and being my home base and my whole heart. Professors Ellen Samuels, Chris Garlough-Shah, Keisha Lindsay, Pernille Ipsen, Jody Lisberger, Jenn Brandt, Carolyn Betensky, and Winnie Brownell for being wonderful mentors and complete badasses. Bekah Havens, thanks for insisting I move these pictures to their own space. Anisa, Ali Eileen Zeiger, and Abby Napier for the warm welcome and continual support. Martha Fischhoff for her overall cheerleading and for being my hero. Sarah Jackson for staying up late, believing in me when I did not, and remembering Skora. Joy Lewis, Chris King, Krystyn Heide, Maile Wilson, Karen Walrond, Erin Glaser, Eden Kennedy, Rachel Rothenberg, Lea Rubenstein, Nomi Hague, and Rose Kauffman, you are better friends than I deserve. Marianne and Ray Hurley for accepting me as one of your own even after I broke every toilet in your house. Special thanks to every single reader of the Feminist Ryan Gosling blog for being beautiful people with impeccable taste. Ryan Gosling, thanks for your unwavering talent, for being a good sport, and getting me through grad school. And the biggest thanks to my husband, Seth. You've given me one thousand brilliant moments and I can't wait to create thousands more. Thanks for supporting all of my weird ideas over the years, laughing when I dance in the kitchen, listening to my rap tourettes, and, most of all, thanks for putting out on our first date.